IMAGES
of America

ANGELICA,
BELMONT, AND
WELLSVILLE

SAMUEL SEABURY

CANDIDATE FOR GOVERNOR
OF NEW YORK STATE

IMAGES
of America

ANGELICA, BELMONT, AND WELLSVILLE

Robert V. Bogan

ARCADIA
PUBLISHING

Published by Arcadia Publishing
Charleston, South Carolina

Library of Congress Catalog Card Number: 2008922388

For all general information contact Arcadia Publishing at:
Telephone 843-853-2070
Fax 843-853-0044
E-mail sales@arcadiapublishing.com
For customer service and orders:
Toll-Free 1-888-313-2665

Visit us on the Internet at www.arcadiapublishing.com

Contents

Acknowledgments

The author would like to thank the following people for their assistance: Craig Braak of Almond, Frank O'Brien of Scio, and Robert McNinch, Richard Miess, Ruth Czankus, and Mary C. Bogan, all of Belmont.

Introduction

If one wanted to go back to the nineteenth century—to live in a frame home, built with planks sawed out of native chestnut—then Angelica would be the place to go. Except for the modern school, the utilities, and the paved roads, this is a community that looks like it did a hundred years ago. Industrialization, shopping malls, and extensive medical centers have turned their backs on this village and this is the way the population wants it. To live here is to live close to the time of the Senecas. The settlers came into this peaceful valley and carved out a community with churches, civic services, shops, and residences, all within walking distance from the village circle. At one time, the county court graced the circle, as Angelica was the county seat before it was moved to Belmont. Imagine what the Indians thought or felt as their native forest was destroyed, their game—upon which they depended for food and clothing—was slaughtered by settlers, and their hunting trails were turned into roadways. Now the descendants of these settlers are threatened, as were the Senecas, by the intrusion of strangers bringing in ash and trash to destroy their peace and quiet and violate the environmental value of their land. What they have had for generations is being taken away.

The history of Belmont is closely connected with and dependent upon the history of the Phillipsburg Mill Reserve. The existence of fine waterpower fostered the commercial prosperity and status of the town. The waterpower induced the first settlers in the present village to locate where they did, and the sale of lots adjoining the reserve gave the village its start. Later, waterpower providers enabled a variety of businesses to be located in the area. Waterpower has been the community's element of promise: it brought men of enterprise to the place and enabled the growth of manufacturers who made its name known throughout the union.

The first settler in the township of Wellsville—as well as the first in Allegany County—was Nathaniel Dyke of Connecticut, who graduated from Yale and served on Washington's staff. He built a cabin along the stream that has been known as Dyke's Creek ever since. The village of Wellsville on the Genesee River was not settled until 1831. At that time a score of settlers met to select a name for the community. They decided on Wellsville because Wells, legend tells us, was the name of the only resident not present at the meeting. About one hundred years ago, there was an attempt to change the village's name to Genesee.

Allegany County is named after an old Indian river—spelled "Allegheny"—that does not cross one inch of the area's soil. It is the smallest of the four western counties of the southern tier in area (1,048 square miles) and in population. (43,000). It is also the highest. The "roof" of the southern tier reaches its apex in Alma Hill, 2,548 feet above sea level. Running the length and breath of old Allegany, the hills stand guard, scalloped against the sky, all the way from Centerville to Ceres, from Short Track to Shongo.

Even from the highest peaks come bumper crops, especially of potatoes and milk. In this rugged land is the spring—known to the Indians long before the arrival of European settlers— whose oil-laden waters provided the first source of petroleum in America. The first test well in New York state was driven deep into the Allegany earth. For three-quarters of a century, the county's buckled terrain has yielded this liquid treasure, and Allegany County leads the Empire State in the production of oil and natural gas.

Allegany's thick woods and quiet hills are the delight of deer hunters. Back in the hills there are roads so remote that the passing of any automobile, other than the rural mail carrier, is an event. Paradoxically, this same county is the only one in the western part of the tier to boast two centers of higher education.

Allegany is Indian country; along the Genesee stood the southernmost village of the Senecas. The natural beauty and power of this area make it a treasure in the American landscape.

One

Angelica

The man on the roof of this schoolhouse, cleaning the chimney, indicates that the school is blessed with central heat in the form of a potbellied stove. The pile of wood by the front door and the lack of leaves on the trees are sure signs that winter is near.

Note the little outhouse, peeking over the fence. The long, cold long walk to this building in the winter was probably not very welcome. Think of the students' struggle with the strict teacher, and the arduous commute in the absence of yellow school buses. Nevertheless, the pupils were able to survive, and some advanced to institutions of higher learning. Some of these early schoolhouses still exist in the county today.

This is the teacher's "tin lizzie." It was not very comfortable in a driving rain, there was not much room for more than two, and the trunk space could hardly take on much luggage. It had wooden-spoked wheels and no front bumper, but it got the teacher there that day.

"I was your queen in calico." How mother had to work to keep our little girl dressed up! All sewing was done by hand, as there were no department stores. The girls had only one good dress for Sunday and for parties, but in the end they really did look like queens.

This is a typical sawmill of the early twentieth century. Notice how the buildings were built. The roof and sides were made of planks, but these were not sawed off to any specific size, just picked up and nailed on. The scrap wood was cast about. If a fire happened to start, there was no hope of saving anything.

Here is a real touring car. It had solid wheels, and the extra tire was not mounted on a wheel. What a chore to change a flat—no automobile club and no phone with which to call! The hand pump was a must. Modern features included a gauge on the radiator, a bumper, and an extended sunshade.

Are you ready for a jaunt in the country? There are three full-size windows on each side, and there is enough running board for the whole crew. There is no spare tire but the sun visor is generous.

This is the birthplace of Irene Ackerman. Irene was the wife of an Allegany County lawyer and judge. The photograph, dated June 8, 1913, shows the couple's homestead. (Photograph courtesy of Carol Mosher.)

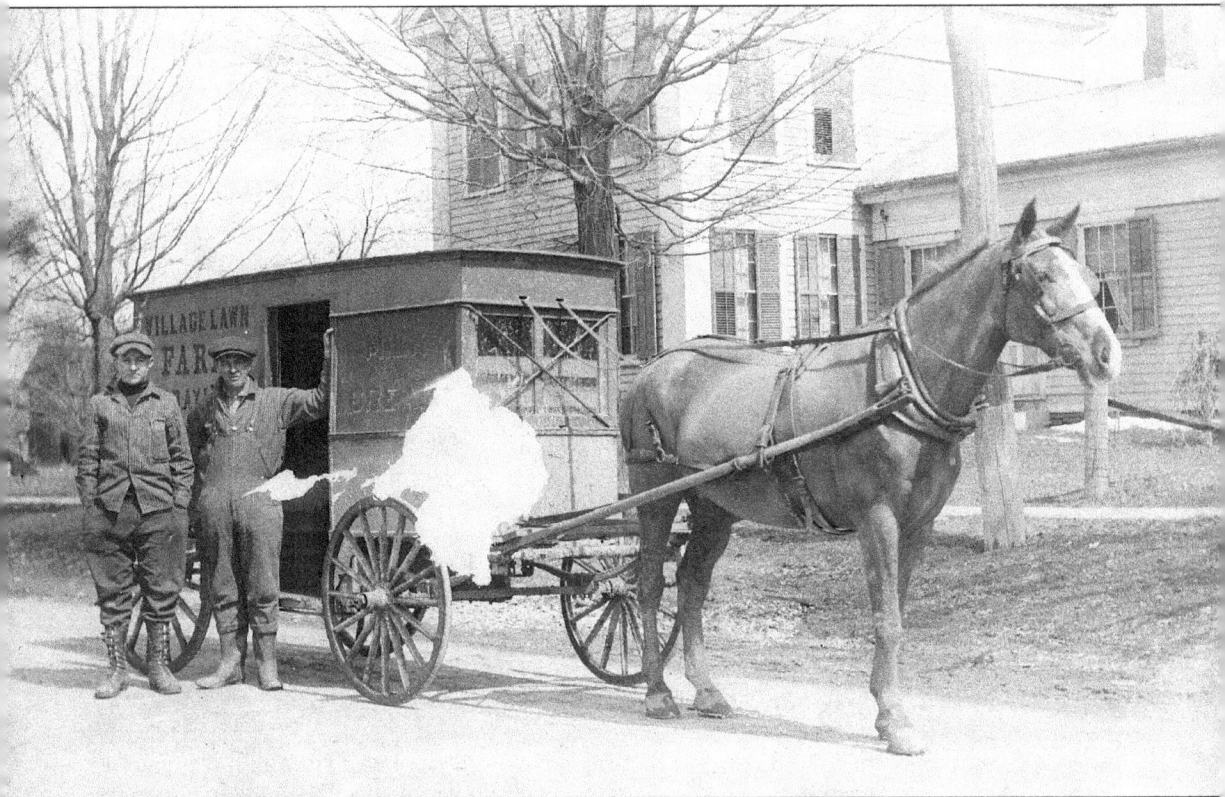

Note the solid iron wheels on this delivery truck. The driver is fully enclosed in the cab and has no side windows. He must rely on the "horse sense" of the animal that pulls the wagon. The driver's warm clothing indicates it must be cold out, but this does not seem to bother either the horse or the attendant.

Angelica members of the Grand Army of the Republic are shown here. They all had memories of those who did not return from the war . . . Some veterans wrote about their fallen comrades, but these records were long ago buried in basements and are now available only to historians.

The Spanish-American War had just faded into the past when this picture was taken. Some of those veterans were still around, but they belonged to an earlier era. At the time this photograph was taken the Kaiser had promised the German people a "place in the sun." American armies lined up to put a damper on his plans.

16

The Allegany County Home was called "the poor house."

This picture captures the former glory of Angelica, then the county seat. A modern courthouse was built on the circle. Notice the dirt road and a pole to carry wires—modern technology was starting to bud.

A house of worship was on the circle in Angelica. Notice that there appear to be some small trees nearby. The church is still there, but the trees are no longer small.

Observe that the horse seems to be in no hurry to get anyplace. The shops are quaint and the men are at ease. No women are in sight.

This quiet pastime was enjoyed while the women were about their chores (surely the ladies would not enjoy an afternoon in the park when they could stay at home sewing, washing, minding the brood, working in the garden, or canning).

RUINS COUNTY HOME
ANGELICA N.Y.
MARCH 15 1923

A lack of adequate communications and fire-fighting equipment often resulted in devastating consequences for these dry, tinderbox buildings. A severe handicap in this March 15, 1923 conflagration was the fact that the building was located outside of the village, in a remote area.

This view of the inside of the postal service depicts a much different facility than one might see today. In the absence of trucks or rural carriers, individuals came by to pick up their mail.

This storm damage occurred on May 16, 1916. The building was ripped apart and nothing was left behind.

Hotels were important features of these rural areas for traveling salesmen. A visit to a local rural area usually required a two-day trip. This hotel still adorns the center of the village.

It was unusual for a small village like Angelica to have two large hotels. Since visitors had no alternative but to stay the night, however, plenty of room was required.

Train derailments were rather common. There were inadequate safety inspections and very often buildings were built close to the tracks.

Store windows needed shading. Observe the small car that has taken advantage of the ample parking space.

A few cars appear here together with horse-drawn rigs and a buggy. The scene depicts a lack of the hustle and bustle common in a big city.

There was plenty of high water around the circle, and the water was just as tranquil as the village since there was nothing around to make waves.

This building represents an improvement over the one-room schoolhouse, but it would clearly not live up to today's standards. Since there is no outhouse in sight, one assumes that the plumbing was inside.

The county home is shown here in its better days. Notice the crates in the foreground that were used for the harvest. The county was able to make a saving in this manner. Such activities, at the present time, would be unacceptable.

THE BRIDGES OF ANGELICA N·Y·

OLEAN STREET

JONCY GORGE

CENTER STREET

MILL POND

...ER ROAD

These bridges were a necessity for rural mobility. Even today, the loss of a bridge spells disaster for the community on the side opposite the town center. In a matter of seconds, they are deprived of access to schools, health facilities, fire protection, and postal services.

Falls and Cascades from Joncy gorge.

Further down the river were the falls and a bridge. Notice how all the bridges utilize a superstructure. These supports are now being replaced with a span under the pavement. The bridge here was important because it afforded access to the mill.

Live musical entertainment was popular before the introduction of tapes, compact discs, and television.

There are no wires or people in this shot, just mud, buildings, and one horse.

Even though this looked like the ultimate facility at the time, it would now be considered too small for use as a school.

It looks like the historic courthouse is getting a facelift. Notice the displacement of dirt, which is the first sign of reconstruction.

There was never a need to hurry on a beautiful summer day.

Notice the mud in this street scene. How did these residents keep the mud out of their houses?

Today we long for the days of the horse and buggy. There were no light bills, no phone bills, and no water and sewer fees.

This beautiful, quiet street symbolizes the tranquility of Angelica.

Angelica, New York, is a place many people are proud to call their home.

Two

Belmont

The American Legion, founded in France after World War I, became the largest veterans' organization. Veterans of other wars have been added to their rolls, and those of World Wars I and II are represented here. Andrew Guidarelli, Garret Casterline, Leo Pike, Bert Thomas, Dave Witter, and Harold Tompkins stand in front of the old legion home, long since demolished and replaced with a modern building.

An old fire-and-steam locomotive crosses the Genesee River in Belmont. There were two terminals in Belmont after the railroads were established, one in Belvidere and the other in Phillipsville. As the towns and villages were established in Allegany County, the railroads expanded. They provided transportation in these small towns and the settlers relied upon them to get supplies and sell their goods. Families who had been separated were able to keep together by using the railroads. Take notice of the two bridges. The one down river is supported by a superstructure, while the one that carries this train uses a flat span.

On March 27, 1908, this mass of twisted steel confronted the railroad men of Belmont. Much of the cleanup was done by manual labor, but eventually the railroad had to send in wrecking equipment. The tracks had to be rebuilt. Oddly enough, there was never an investigation to see who was at fault; it mattered not. There were quite a few railroad men on pensions, but even this source of income from the railroad has disappeared today.

Nav. 7. 09

Another train wreck occurred on November 7, 1909. In small villages today, the railroads are a part of the past. Some old railroad stations have been converted into residences and some have been left to deteriorate, abandoned for a lack of business. The railroad industry could not compete with truckers, who could deliver to the doors of their customers and who did not have to maintain tracks or emergency crews.

Train derailments caused a great deal of damage. They held up schedules and injured—and sometimes killed—employees. Nevertheless, the railroads provided employment to many of the families in the small communities in Allegany County. Many sons followed in their fathers' footsteps and received good jobs, and the railroad companies relied on this source of labor. A career on the rails involved dangerous, hard work, but these men had strong backs and a willing spirit. The jobs were treasured because they paid well. As the roads were built, some of the laborers dropped off and settled in these towns. Most were immigrants—primarily Italians and Irish—and had little education. Some were in the country illegally, but they stayed.

A typical plank home in Belmont is shown as it appears today. Shutters were a vital means of preserving the home in the 1840s, when this house was built. Today they are ornamental.

Dotted around this small town are dairy farms. Many dairy farmers were descendants of the railroad workers who settled here; they were encouraged to move west to grow crops in the rich soil of Allegany County. When they got here, they saw the hills and the stony soil, and realized that with the cold there would be a slow growing season. They did not give up, and used the land instead to raise sheep and cattle. The trains made their products marketable. These family farms were viable until young sons were lured away to pursue other careers.

The town fathers feared the black smoke from the Clark Brothers Foundry would settle on their beautiful white homes. When the foundry burned after a fire, the town would not permit the brothers to rebuild "because they did not want those men, with their dirty clothes and dinner pails, walking around the streets of our nice clean village." The Clark Brothers moved, with their tax money, to Olean and prospered.

This dam in downtown Belmont was made of planks. What a delight it was to the residents! Children and adults swam in the cool water during the summer and ice-skated in the winter. Ice was cut for the icebox and stored for summer use. In the spring and summer, residents fished and picnicked on the east bank and the small island. The firemen arranged a carnival here in the late summer. The bridge over Schuyler Street has been replaced by a modern structure today.

Pub. by Charles E. Mills.

Free Library, Belmont, N

This library was in use during the Spanish-American War. The present generation of patrons that uses the building sits in the same seats that their great-grandparents once did. What a benefit this is to the community! It has guaranteed the availability of great works by Longfellow, Emerson, and others to all residents. The library staff performed a labor of love in the early days, keeping up the facility without compensation. No one thought of being paid, since the pleasure derived from the work was pay enough. Even today, there are those who volunteer their time at the library for the benefit of many.

Huge sums were paid to build the superstructures that supported the bridges, providing work for iron foundries all over the land. Railroads were considered benefactors, providing work, transportation, and truly the wheels of commerce. Actually, when the chips were down and they were no longer turning a profit, the railroads became costly to the taxpayers.

All local farmers maintained ice houses. The plank dam at Belmont was utilized by the local residents as a source of free ice in the winter. The weather did the work of making the ice, and a hardy person with a strong back cut the blocks into cubes of approximately 100 pounds each and put them into the ice houses. The cubes were separated by sawdust or fodder to prevent them from freezing together.

42

This park does not look like the one that is in the same location today. The big Civil War cannon is no longer there, its present whereabouts unknown. During World War II there was a shortage of metal, and those who were concerned with the shortage canvassed small towns looking for scrap metal and convinced the local magistrates that it was their patriotic duty to donate such relics to the war effort. Having acquired the item, the metal collectors sold it to scrap dealers at a handsome profit. It is possible that the Civil War cannon was sacrificed in such a misguided effort. The park is now circular, and contains a large monument to the Civil War veterans and a watering trough for horses (now largely unused).

Labor Day, Sep 4, 1911 ~ Belmont, N.Y.

Oh for the life of a volunteer fireman! They put out fires, saved people, got cats out of trees, put a first-class shine on all the equipment, kept the fire hall clean, and kept their uniforms pressed. The firemen are shown here on Labor Day in 1911. The units strove to defeat those of neighboring communities in regular firemen's competitions. Notice the long gowns of the ladies. Were they able to keep these clean even when the dirt streets were wet and muddy? The poles supporting wires in front of the building are now gone, the street is paved, and the proud hotel has become a bar.

The man in the foreground offers lunch buckets for the crew. The trains provided the only means of transportation between cities and villages. The days of the stagecoach and the pony express vanished with the arrival of the Iron Horse. Note the real horse and the delivery wagon behind the railroad station, which were used to transport goods to locations off the tracks.

The awning manufacturers enjoyed a brisk business years ago, but where are these sun shields today? Perhaps because of the high level of maintenance these accessories required—they were rolled out daily, buttoned on the side, and withdrawn quickly in foul weather—they were eliminated as time passed. Air conditioning became the means of protecting the store from extreme heat.

Public music instruction was provided by these minstrels, just as it was in the twelfth century. With musical instruments, these performers wandered about singing the songs of the times, stopping in the park or perhaps at the local watering hole as the patrons drank and listened. These entertainers were likely to appear at a farmer's back door and trade a few songs for table scraps, and the children were always delighted to see them. Notice the tin cup on the pedestal.

This wonderful estate exists today, but is very difficult to see from the road. The land was acquired by Phillip Church from his father, Richard Church, in 1800. Angelica, named after Phillip's daughter, was surveyed by Mr. Church and Indian fighter Moses Van Campan. The building was constructed from sandstone and lumber from the native trees. The county is proud of this estate and the lives of the family that occupied it for generations.

The Allegany County Courthouse is shown here on June 23, 1907. The second floor was occupied by the county judge, who served as the county's social service department. He took care of the homeless, the poor, the ill, and the aged, and managed Potter's Field.

The sheriff's office and county jail were also located in the courthouse. The sheriff's wife was the matron who fed the prisoners. The sheriff, who claimed the protection of the king, often had the prisoners perform manual labor, shoveling snow or tending livestock in town.

By the time this photograph was taken, just a few years before World War II, paved streets and sidewalks had replaced the dirt roads and horses of the previous generation. The small building in the foreground was the location of the *Amity Press*. It is still in operation but does not print a daily paper as it did in those days, perhaps because readers lost interest in reading articles about such subjects as "Aunt Irene, from East Rochester, where, she works as the chief sampler in the sauerkraut factory, her sister says she shows in her facial expressions, will be visiting her brother John on West Triana Terrace, for a day and a half. All were delighted as she left." A desire for less provincial news coverage, combined with the growing availability of papers from Rochester and Buffalo, lead to the demise of the local paper. The post office was located in the building to the north, which has been replaced by a new building.

Stores lined Schuyler Street in the late 1920s. The corner grocery was operated by an Italian immigrant who came to Belmont after working for the railroad in Belfast. At the outset of World War I, he enlisted in the United States Army. After his honorable discharge, he returned to Belmont and kept the store for the rest of his working life. On the same street were Candyland, a dime store, a tailor, and a shoemaker. Now they are all gone.

It looks like there is another holiday arriving since the hotel has its bunting out. The population in the small towns took holidays seriously.

As the holidays became part of the benefits of the union contract, they were treated as personal luxuries and the true meanings of those days were lost. They were also exploited by the merchants, who used them as days to hold special sales.

There was definitely no organization that was more respected than that of the volunteer firemen. They risked their lives to save the property and lives of their neighbors. When the alarm was sounded, they dropped what they were doing and ran off to the fire in great haste. In many villages the homes were close together, so there was a great risk of fire spreading and multiple buildings being burned. The firemen treated rich and poor alike, and entered any burning building to save people and their pets. Without modern equipment, brute strength was used to fight the flames.

Here, the firemen's parade is forming. The parade was usually accompanied with an outdoor picnic.

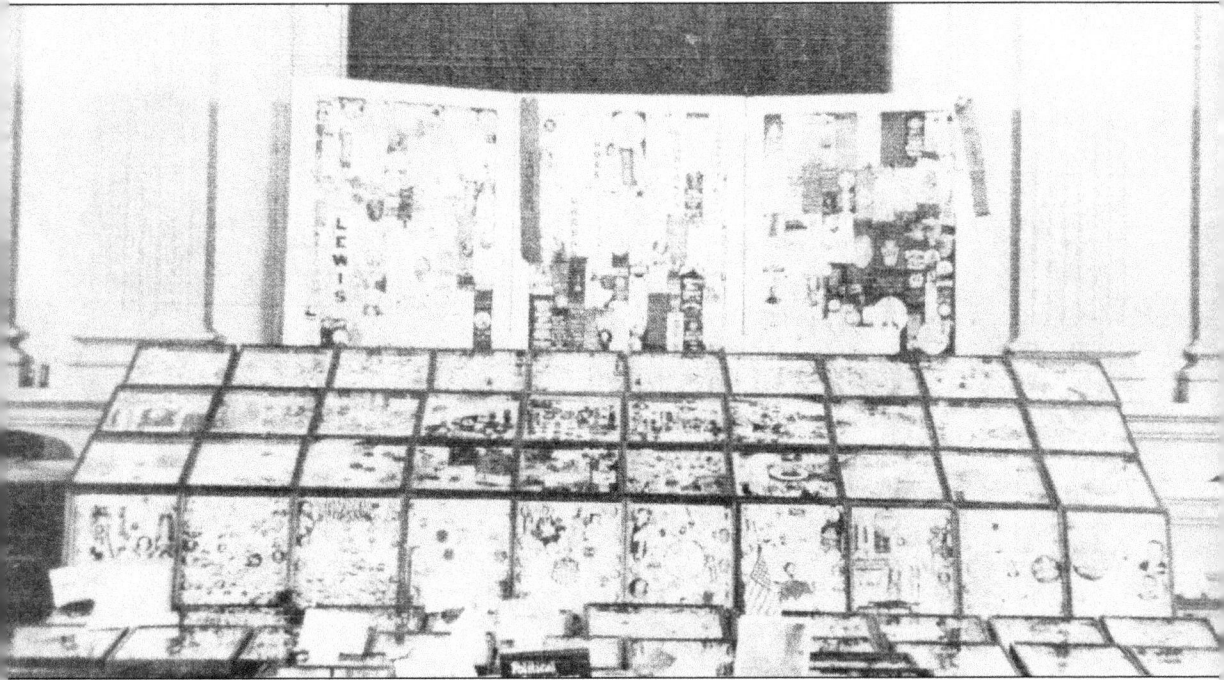

Very few thought of collecting the political paraphernalia that documented the progress of local and national elections. Our ancestors did not realize the value of these materials to historians in later years.

Mighty and proud, on the crest of the hill, stands the county court. All the affairs of the citizens were subject to the stern judgment of a county judge and jury system.

This span across the Genesee River lacks the usual extensive superstructure. The river looks shallow at this point, but it rises in the spring when the snow melts and the water comes off the hills. Great floods once occurred along the Genesee; these are now held in check by a dam at Mount Morris and another dam at Rushford Lake. The power company that owns the Rushford Lake dam has determined to let the cottage-dwellers along the lake maintain it.

The bitterness of the American Revolution was still felt in the early 1800s. Homes were deliberately built in the Colonial style in order to avoid association with England or the Tories. Tories were treated rather harshly in those days. Their lands and homes were confiscated and, if they would not leave of their own accord, they were tarred and feathered and driven out of town. As we tour these villages, notice the styles of the homes.

The Belmont Hotel, designed by Charles Whitney, was majestic in its day. Fortunately there were a lot of strong backs available to carry the bricks and mortar to erect this building. Every rural community needed such a hotel to accommodate traveling salesmen, politicians, men of the cloth, lawyers, judges, and honored guests. Local people also supported the hotel by using it as a meeting place and by patronizing its bar.

A new building was constructed for the county surrogate, who cared for the poor, the disabled, and the aged. Economic conditions such as the decline of the dairy industry, the reduction of railroad service, the national depression, and business failures all added up to more work for the surrogate's office. In addition, many county records were kept by the surrogate over the years; these could not be destroyed and more storage space was needed. Little did the founding fathers realize that the expansion of social services, the probation department, child support units, and the health department would make even the current space inadequate. The present lawn must give way to parking lots, but how long will it be before the parking lots must give way to new buildings?

The farming community depended on the daily milk pickup provided by the milk plants. When milk-processing equipment changed and it was no longer possible for the milk plants to make pickups on so many dirt roads, dairy farmers turned to raising beef cattle. This reduced the amount of milk being processed at the milk plant. Eventually, the plants closed and Belmont farmers had to rely on refrigerated trucks.

In many local areas there were cheese plants that utilized the surplus milk. They were very secretive about their operation and produced a good product, which they took to the markets in Buffalo and Rochester. For a while, as the milk plants began to close, the cheese plants did a good business. Unfortunately, they also proved unable to compete with the large plants erected by American interests in Cuba and New York City, and they eventually fell to modernization.

55

Most schools supported a band, instilling in students a love of music. After these young musicians left school, they joined local bands and usually played in all the town parades and at festive events. Who were these talented band members? Just locals from Snowball Hollow Road, or one of the farms up Hood Hill. They had little to do with their spare time after the chores were done. They joined the lads from South Street and Milton Street and practiced. On Sunday afternoon, weather permitting, they appeared on the bandstand and entertained the citizens of the village. Some adopted the military style and paraded at most conventions for the firemen and political rallies. The bands were appreciated but crowds declined after the advent of radio.

For those who lost their lives, it didn't matter how large the battle was or which side triumphed in the end. These men were proud of their service in a long and grueling war.

In its days as a farming community, Belmont actually supported some farms in the village itself. Observe the barn (it was painted red) and the horse-drawn wagon on the right side of the photograph. The scene at this location is different now: it is more commercial. A huge building occupies the vacant lot and the boardwalks have been replaced with sidewalks. The farming element has been removed and the mud street is now paved.

A farm home looked like this in the days before lawn mowers were used. Grass was usually tended by the family sheep and chickens. The apple tree on the right was a valuable asset to the farmer. Money was too hard to come by for the farmer to squander it on anything that he could grow himself. The tree provided apples and hard cider.

On the road between Belmont and Mainville (an unmapped settlement) there stood the home of one Fred Daley, a resident of Irish descent. Fred's home, once featured in Ripley's Believe It or Not, utilized license plates for siding and roofing. Fred and the home are long gone, but it still stands in the memories of natives. This picture was loaned to me by Robert McNinch, who can recall Fred walking back and forth to Belmont.

Three

Wellsville

This photograph and the following four photographs show the development of the oil fields in Wellsville. The tax money generated, the employment of thousands (both in the fields and in the refinery), and the personal wealth of the owners and investors created an enthusiasm equal to that of the gold rush. The first hint of this excitement appears in the Beers' *The History of Allegany County*, which quotes a June 21, 1879 report in the *Elmira Gazzette* of "the decided success of Mr. O.P. Taylor's enterprise, in boring for petroleum."

The following excerpt about Wellsville and its oil fields was written by Arch Merrell in his book *Southern Tier*:

The following from the *Elmira Gazette* of June 21, 1879, was received as the last pages of this work were about to go to press [and concern] the decided success of O.P. Taylor's enterprise in boring for petroleum. "There is no disguising the fact that oil has been found in Wellsville and in paying quantities. Triangle Well . . . four and one miles southwest from Wellsville . . . was commenced April 17 . . . At 1,109 feet the oil-bearing sand was reached . . . The drill stopped at 1,317. On June 12 the Well was torpedoed with a twenty quart shot of glycerin when the oil was sent 20 to 30 feet over the derrick. Saturday came the flow since which time there has flowed between 8 and 10 barrels a day. The well is certainly a gusher. Sunday brought a crowd. The place was named Triangle City. Four lager beer stands were started. The town was filling up with strangers. Letters, telegrams, and inquiries were pouring in. Look out for the great big city at Wellsville."

The editor showed sound judgment in making that breathless last minute addition to *The History of Allegany County*. The "gusher" at Triangle City in June of 1879 was one of the most significant events in Allegany County's history. It ushered in a new and golden age, especially for Wellsville and the southern tier of towns. It also brought in the wildest, most hell-roaring period in the history of the county. Arch Merrell continues in *Southern Tier*:

Taylor's Triangle No. 1 in the Town of Scio made history. It was the first productive commercial well in Allegany County. It started a mad boom. Triangle City sprang up where there had been a barren field. Derricks began to dot the countryside.

Orville P. Taylor, the man who started it all, had been making and selling cigars in Wellsville before he went into the oil business. He put down two wells that were failures before he hit the jackpot with Triangle No. 1. He had put all he had, and all that he could borrow, into drilling. His wife sold her jewelry to raise money to complete the venture. During the Second World War the memory of this oil pioneer who would not give up—who has been called "The Colonel Drake of the Allegany field"—was honored by the federal government when it named a Liberty ship the *Orville P. Taylor*.

The following excerpt was also taken from *Southern Tier*:

The oil madness reached its apogee in Richburg in 1881. That village, named after a settler and widout [sic] any prophetic allusion, had slept the years away on the shady road that led over the hills between Bolivar and Friendship. [Author's note: Friendship was originally called Bloody Corners.] It had 25 buildings and less than 200 inhabitants . . .

Out of the madness of the boom days, Wellsville emerged as the capital of the Allegany oil fields, one of the most prosperous, substantial [areas] in Upper New York, with a population of nearly 6,500. Wellsville shrugs off oil depressions. As long as the oil pumps chug away in the hills around it and the pipelines bring the crude to the huge Sinclair refinery in the oil capital, Wellsville's economy will remain as solid as old South Hill, the 2,300 foot high gate keeper at the end of its principal street.

The generosity of the wealthy was evidenced by their support of the Salvation Army. Even in the depression of the thirties, Wellsville and Allegany County were able to prevent catastrophes of starvation and dispossession. The Salvation Army operated without fanfare and many families today do not know that their grandparents would not have been able to survive without their help.

This spotless structure was located on Wellsville's main street. With all the business that was generated by the oil fields, the industries, and banking and service operations, there was a great need for hotel space. Time has taken its toll on this beautiful enterprise. As the roads improved and the automobile shortened the time needed to traverse the distance between cities, the need for overnight rooms and elaborate dining menus was lessened.

"Wellsville City Hall" was a true misnomer. Wellsville never became a city. Despite all the money that the oil industry poured into the area, the landscape remained rural. This was due to the will of the people—rich and poor—and it remains true today. Recently, however, the cost of operating the village became more than the taxpayers could bear. The loss of the revenue from the oil giants and the loss of taxes from and service of the railroads have placed the cost of operating a village administration beyond the reach of the middle-class property owners. In addition, many town services have been duplicated by the county and state. Already some of the surrounding villages and communities have dissolved and taken the status of hamlets. The city hall shown in the photograph has long since been torn down.

Would these days ever give way to modernization? Telephones did not have push buttons and there were no 800 numbers. Instead, we completed our calls through a local telephone operator: "Hey Mabel, this is Tom. Get me Henry at the bank." No one or thing will ever replace Mabel! The automobile was still called the horseless carriage, but kids were already calling it a car. It shared the road with horses and people. The automobile shown here takes up its share of the road (driving right down the middle!) and the driver operates it from the right side.

The First Methodist Episcopal Church was organized in 1830 and built at a cost of $2,000. The pastor was Reverend Azel N. Fillmore. There were thirteen families in the parish and the church installed the first bell in Wellsville in 1853. In 1854 the town clock was installed in the church's tower. When this photograph was taken, there were still plank sidewalks to help those crossing the road fend off the mud. The building is still standing today.

St. John's Episcopal Church was founded in 1859 as a mission of the Diocese of Western New York. The organization remained a mission until April 27, 1866, when it was recognized as a parish. On August 13 of the same year, the cornerstone of the new church was laid. The cost of the church was almost $4,000 dollars. The building then stood on Jefferson Street behind the railroad tracks, but in 1872 parishioners moved it to the lot on which it now stands at a cost of $600.

The prosperity of the village was dependent on various shops. Sawmills were popular and lucrative, but when lumber became scarce the mills moved to other locations. Foundry workers cherished their jobs, but many detested the black dirt from the foundry that attached itself to clothes and skin, and even affected the internal organs. Prior to the discovery of oil, village tanneries were the prime target for expansion. Tanneries produced a foul odor, discolored the skin of their workers, and damaged the workers' senses of smell, taste, and sight. Nevertheless, support for the tanneries remained strong.

In the beginning of the twentieth century, some dreamed that man would leave the face of the earth and take to the skies. The Ford V-8 had not yet hit the streets, but those with great vision and enterprise began to look to the future—would it one day be possible to traverse the ocean without a ship?

The airport in Wellsville, which was developed by private enterprise, originally lacked radar. Although it is not a regular stop for commercial airlines, the Wellsville Airport is able to service lighter craft. Connections are made to Buffalo, Rochester, Elmira, Jamestown, and Bradford. You can leave Wellsville and arrive in London, Paris, or Rome!

Once the railroad arrived in Wellsville, people came from all directions: passengers arrived and departed, and freight needed to be handled. Note the carriage at the left end of the station. The three stacks service stoves that were located in different parts of the building. These burned quite a bit of fuel during the winter, which often brought consecutive days of sub-zero temperatures. Today the building is empty. No trains stop here; in fact, most of the track has been torn up to lower tax liability.

On this busy day in Wellsville, a delivery man in full uniform is about to serve the customer waiting on the sidewalk on the other side of the street. Even though the street is paved and curbs have been installed, the horse shares the right-of-way with the automobile. There are no power lines or gaslight street lamps in sight; their day has not yet arrived.

This metal processing plant was relatively new in the early twentieth century. Producing lightweight parts for the aircraft industry and the medical profession, it brought employment and taxes into an already thriving village. Apparently no foundry work was done on site; castings were reportedly made in the Drake Brothers shop in Friendship.

At this time, automobile manufacturers did not yet see the advantage of reducing the weight of automobile parts and did not utilize the services of plants like this one; only later did the industry determine that weight was related to the consumption of gasoline and rust prevention.

David A. Howe was born in West Almond on July 26, 1848. He grew up in Wellsville, where his father was the editor of the local newspaper. After his marriage, he moved to Pennsylvania, where he made his fortune in the lumber business. His aunt, Louise Brown, was president of the Monday Club, a ladies' literary club that started a library in Wellsville. Mr. Howe became interested in his aunt's project and built the first Howe Library in 1910. When he died in 1925, he left the bulk of his fortune—over one million dollars—as an endowment to the present library.

Money for the construction of the present library came from ten years' accrued interest on the endowment left by Mr. Howe. The roof of the library is shingled with handmade clay tiles, and there are flagstone terraces in the front and back of the building. Originally there were extensive lawns from the back of the building to the river. The Georgian Colonial-style building, begun in 1935 and opened in 1937, was designed by A.D. Ade of Rochester and built by the L.C. Whitford Company of Wellsville.

The residence of E.C. Bradley typified the many homes of wealthy oil men, who were benefactors of the village and the county both because of the tax revenue they provided and because of their charitable contributions. Our school system, one of the best in western New York, could not have been built or sustained without their help. This group of wealthy oil men had a very deep sense of responsibility to the village and county and paid heed to the welfare of those who worked for them and their families. They provided funding for all types of intellectual and recreational benefits.

MARATHON RESTAURANT, WELLSVILLE, N.Y.

For over 75 years, this has been the location of the Texas Hot, a gathering place dear to many residents of this little village. The present owners of the Texas Hot recently celebrated the restaurant's 75th year of operation with all of the booths in their original positions. Everyone who lives in Wellsville has an affinity to this establishment. Early faithful patrons—who came for breakfast, lunch, and dinner—believed this to be their home and treated it as such. Returning veterans of World War II made a beeline to the Texas Hot before they unpacked. Ask anyone!

Little did those who walked past by this firm realize that it would provide a living for their children and grandchildren, and now for their great-grandchildren, boys and girls alike. No one dreamed that women would work in shops. Grover Cleveland, the sheriff of Erie County to the north, was opposed to women getting out of the kitchen and would be shocked to see how this business evolved. Dresser Industries continues to provide employment today.

The Genesee River originates from a hill of springs just a little south of Genesee, Pennsylvania. The hills in Allegany County are steep and are often snow-bound. When melting snow is combined with rain, flooding can be expected. This picture is not really unusual, and it shows what unruly water can do.

74

It's off to the races! Wellsville, with all its oilmen and industries, would not be denied its days to relax and enjoy the sport of kings. The days of racing were short and hardly anyone became an addict with such limited exposure. Buoyed by the sunshine, however, quite a few dollars would change hands at the races.

Along with these events in Wellsville, there were the races at the county fair in Angelica. What a sad happening to raise a horse, train it, pay its board and caretaker for an entire year, and then tote it over to Angelica only to watch it run its best and come in a loser.

These three young men in their touring caps are enjoying what today would be called an antique automobile. Isn't it remarkable that all automobiles were painted black? It seems that it did not dawn on anyone that it was possible to paint the machine any other color until about 1928, when more women gradually became drivers. At that point, more colors we used. During a period from the 1930s to the 1960s, family cars were even painted with two or more colors.

Wellsville's parks, one of which appears in this photograph, were quiet places to stroll and observe the flora and birds. They were built by the village and were put to good use before television arrived and kept people inside. Monuments to veterans and civic personalities adorned these recreational areas.

This photograph, taken at the intersection of Main and Pearl Streets, shows a group of people undaunted by a rainstorm. Not a cover for the drays and automobiles is in sight. There is no traffic light or traffic policeman at the intersection. Who, pray tell, prevented accidents?

The three ladies in front of the Fasset Hotel are about to tip-toe through the horse droppings, a daily event no doubt. There are no street lights but telephone wires are plentiful. The horses seem to carry the day, but soon they would vanish from the road. Think of how they would struggle against the tractor-trailers we see on the road toady. The men in the automobiles with their derby hats would likewise have quite a struggle.

Look at the big town in the 1940s. A chain store, the bane of the small shopkeeper, was located right downtown. There was a three-phase traffic light, and crosswalks were painted on the street. Streetlights had appeared and a village coffee shop served shoppers and businessmen. Where are the rugged oil workers? The refinery is gone, and the oil workers have been replaced by well-suited gentlemen with tender hands.

The driver of the automobile in the foreground, who is driving without a license plate attached to the rear of his car, is about to steer into the middle of the street. Let there be no doubt about it. The gentlemen enjoying a conversation in the middle of the highway will be required to give way. It looks as if the approaching driver has already conceded.

Without traffic lights, police officers, or center lines, many drivers felt they owned the roads. The only one that appears to be safe is that soul with his straw hat and bicycle. There probably will come a day when he will be required to fight for his share of the road.

Here stands the Fassett Hotel, with its two balconies. Isaac W. Fassett was born in Springfield on February 18, 1815. In 1850 he came to Wellsville, where he was engaged in lumbering until 1870, giving employment to twenty men. He built extensively, and owned 6,000 acres of real estate. In the spring of 1878, he became involved in the grocery trade. He served the town of Wellsville for two years as supervisor and served the village as president of the board of education.

The McEwen brothers' machine shop seems to have been able to open up in spite of the heavy snow. It is reported in Beers' *The History of Allegany County* that the business was started by Duncan McEwen in 1861, after he served as the foreman for Smith and Williams. Duncan McEwen died in 1864 and his widow operated the business until 1868. The establishment was then taken over by the couple's two sons. In 1876 it burned to the ground, but it was rebuilt.

Duncan McEwen, the father of the McEwen brothers, was born in Perthshire, Scotland. He came to America in 1849 and settled in Angelica in 1852. In 1856, he began a business for himself on a small scale: a lathe and drilling machine were his starting inventory. In 1861 he bought a lot on Main and State Streets, establishing the first wool carding machine in Wellsville. The business prospered until 1864, the time of his death. The partnership of his two sons continued his work.

The refinery that brought in millions of dollars in wages and profit is now gone. It had its shares of disasters, including the refinery fire of June 17, 1938, and the gas well that ran wild south of Wellsville in 1940. The fire killed three and injured forty-two, and control of the second incident required the expert assistance of specialists from Texas.

But what a disaster it was when the refinery chose to leave Wellsville. The resulting unemployment deprived families of income and security.

The "Coats" sign bears a name important in the development of Wellsville. There are 36 members of the Coats family prominent in local history. W.H. Coats was a "choirister" in the First Baptist choir and a trustee of the first board of trade. When a fire occurred in his residence, the neighbors carried buckets of water and were able to extinguish the flames before the arrival of the firemen. The success of his cabinet shop prevailed to the good fortune of the village.

81

The Genesee, the mighty, northbound river that cuts the state of New York as the Rhine cuts Germany (like the Rhine it is adorned with castles), is a fine trout stream. It flows as gently as England's "Sweet Afton" as it glides through Wellsville. The river is more than a volume of water irrigating its banks and turning mill wheels, more than a blue ribbon woven in the green vesture of the earth. To those who know how it has affected the course of events along its valley for scores of years, it is a source of fascination. To the intrinsic interest of stirring incidents is added the charm of their having occurred on familiar ground. This view is of the now-famous Wellsville Riverwalk, which has been officially designated a New York State Historical Site.

This bridge has not changed since the day the oncoming driver urged his steed to get to the other side, and the need to cross the river remains. The waterway, not always as quiet as it was this day, was not always easy to cross. Not long after this picture was taken, a large school was built on the left to educate the children of the river dwellers. (A photograph of that school appears later.)

In the 1820s much of Wellsville was covered with forest. Twenty years later, there were shops along Main Street, and in the 1850s and 1860s, brick buildings were built to house businesses.

The advent of the automobile and the farm tractor changed the complexion of Main Street. A newspaper and the Marathon Restaurant moved into town, along with a bank and retail merchants.

The Wellsville City Hall is prominent on the left side of the photograph. Most of the principal buildings of the present day were built after the destructive fires of 1867, 1871, and 1872. The building shown here are as follows: the Pioneer Block (built by Fassett and Simmons, 1868); the Central Block (Alexander Smith, H. Alger, and W.H. Plum, 1868–69); Brown's Block (A.S. Brown); the Union Block (E.B. Tullar, Hoyt and Lewis, and E.B. Halland); and the Barnes Block (York & Chamberlain and Judd & Burns).

In the 1830s, the business section of Wellsville began to develop. The town overtook its neighbors both in enterprise and in population, and this growth was to continue. Businessmen like Sam Hills, E.A. Smith, and Harmon Van Buren made significant contributions to the development of commerce in the area, and the town's population swelled from 2,439 inhabitants in 1860 (the year of the first census) to 4,247 in 1875.

Country Club, Wellsville, N.Y. 716

The rich took time off to play at this beautiful, nine-hole golf course. The course was a real challenge for the golfers, and also a work of art. The best of services were available to the club's exclusive members and their families. The most elite weddings and parties were held here in an atmosphere of grandeur and opulence. No expense was spared in the hiring of personnel, technicians, and furnishings. The equipment and maintenance were the best. Happy was the businessman or professional who had time to put aside the cares of the day and indulge.

Not many people ventured onto North Main Street in Wellsville on a day like this—the snow kept most horses and automobiles locked safely in barns. There is one horse-drawn wagon out with two hardy souls aboard, however.

Around this time, a large number of Germans emigrated to the United States. Jacob Rauber and his wife, Elizabeth Thebold, arrived in Wellsville in 1852 from Wittenburg, Prussia; in 1853 Rauber purchased the farm of E.A. Smith, south of the village. These Germans immigrants brought with them some native skills, and their ranks included talented furniture makers from the Black Forest. It is not surprising that the Rauber Furniture establishment was founded in Wellsville. It is visible on the right side of the photograph.

The next four photographs depict the results of the development of a school system in Wellsville. At the 1832 town meeting in Scio (today the village of Wellsville), settlers along the river resolved to raise money to erect a log schoolhouse opposite Simon's Opera House. The school was provided with a mammoth fireplace, similar in style to those in vogue among the Pennsylvania Dutch.

In this primitive schoolhouse, Miss Huldah Hall was duly installed as teacher. It is said that she showed "neither fear nor favor" to her pupils. Reading, writing, arithmetic, geography, and grammar were all part of the curriculum, and "the old practice of teaching and enforcing good manners was regarded as important," according to one who was familiar with the schools of the village at that period.

On April 12, 1859, a resolution was passed to build a new schoolhouse in District #1, and $1,500 of tax money was allotted for that purpose. On December 15, 1859, the superintendent of buildings reported that the schoolhouse was finished and presented his bill for $1,468.50. (The cost of putting in the seats was $370, bringing the total cost of construction to $1838.50.) These buildings, so sturdy and modern in their time, are today overcrowded and obsolete.

At a special meeting in November 1859, a resolution was reached to build a "union free school" in Wellsville. A board of education was then elected; the members were Charles Collins, Hiram York, H.M. Shearer, George W. Russell, William Peebles, W.H. Coats, Edmund Baldwin, W.S. Johnson, and I.W. Fassett. The visions of these men brought about schools like these.

Small transportation corporations were needed to serve villages and towns that were beyond the scope and purposes of the huge railroad, which was focused on large profits generated by volume. These little towns needed some way to haul produce to market and to provide supplies to customers along the way. The W.A.G. Railroad, terminating in Galeton, was the small company that served this area.

In later years, when trucks took over the freight business and buses took care of passengers, these railroads could no longer turn high profits. The station seen in this photograph soon passed away and the right-of-way became a hiking trail.

This was the original David A. Howe Library, built in 1910, fifteen years before his death. Increased acquisitions brought about the need for a new library, which was opened in 1937. The original library now houses the village offices.

After entering the entrance hall, one observes the reading room and reference room of the Howe Library. The paneling in this area is made of riff-swan white oak. The floors are composed of cork strips and the ceilings have been acoustically treated with plaster and hand-molded trim. Overhead, just inside the entrance, there is a skylight that receives light from the cupola on top of the building. Notice the oak Ionic pillars separating the rooms and the hand-carved oak trim. Over the doorways are different carvings representing the Tree of Life, the Lamp of Knowledge, and the Hive of Industry.

The oil portrait of David A. Howe was painted after his death from a photograph by H. Willard Ortlip. The carving around the portrait is the most elaborate in the building. It is of English lime wood, done in the style of Grinling Gibbons, a seventeenth-century English artist.

Here we see the Buffalo and Susquehanna Railroad. The Erie Railroad was not the only one to serve the village of Wellsville, although it was certainly the most significant line to run through this area. There was little growth in the community until the survey of the Erie Railway in 1840 and 1841, at which time there was a considerable influx of strangers. During their sojourn, Wellsville enjoyed a fleeting period of prosperity.

The sanitarium, pictured above, was designed as a kind of nursing home for elderly or infirm wealthy patients who did not rightly belong in hospital wards. The creation of the sanitarium reduced the need for doctors to make house calls and relieved families of the burden of home care. The sanitarium gave dignity to the aged, some of whom were demented or physically unable to care for themselves. It also gave these affluent patients a use for their money, which they gladly spent.

On the left, carriages await the disembarking passengers at this brand-new railroad station. Its tiled roof could withstand two hundred winters. Inside, one could even send a telegraph. The passenger cars that traveled through here were the most comfortable of the day.

Little did these passengers realize, however, that the demise of the railroad was just around the corner. Even the great wealth of an oil community could not save it. Motor transportation and aircraft arrived to carry away passengers and mail contracts.

A photograph of the Whitney Mansion is included in this chapter; even though the mansion is located in Belmont, it is the pride of the entire county.

C.A. Whitney was a well-known craftsman whose talent and energy were used to complete many local buildings. Whitney's legacy has been preserved by the mansion's present owner, Ruth Czankus. She has restored the dwelling to its previous dignity. A tour of the grounds and the building calls to mind the days of yore, when Belmont was a series of small hills. The courthouse is built on top of one of these domes and the Whitney Mansion is atop another, just south of the center of the village. Ms. Czankus relates the interesting history of the builder and the spirits he left behind.

"The Pink House" is located at the corner of West State Street and South Brooklyn Avenue on the west side of town. No person ever recalls seeing this exact color of paint on any other building anywhere (to speak precisely, the shade is mauve or lavender and not truly pink, despite the name the people of Wellsville have given to this house). The residence has worn that spectacular coat ever since it was built over one hundred years ago by the late druggist E.B. Hall. The Hall will stipulated no other color ever be used.

The ornate brick residence is trimmed in white. The driveway is guarded by two angelic figures and the doorway by two lions. Hall's daughter, Mrs. J.M. Carpenter, resided in the house and every Christmas she framed the grounds with many different lights. Local folk tales also report a haunting of the grounds.

This is another view of the Wellsville Sanitarium. It is long gone; today the wealthy share nursing homes with the poor.

This monument is dedicated to all Allegany Civil War veterans, and commemorates the service of Amity Civil War veteran George H. Blakman (born in Pitmouth on April 23, 1841). Married on June 22, 1870, to Alice Rawson of Belmont, Blakman earned great honors on Southern battlefields. He enlisted as a private in Company E of the 93rd Regiment, New York State Volunteers, in September 1861 at the age of twenty, and served the company in all its marches and engagements until the fall of 1863. He re-enlisted and was made orderly sergeant. At the Battle of the Wilderness, he was wounded in five places, one ball passing through his breast and another entering his right arm near the shoulder, severing an artery and breaking the bones in many places. He walked from the battlefield to Fredericksburg, a distance of 18 miles, and it was eight days before he received any surgical treatment. His right arm was amputated. He returned to his company as its commander and participated in the grand review.

Erie Depot, Wellsville, N. Y.

In this last view of Wellsville, a beautiful matched team pulls a carriage through town. A lone conductor stands ready to convey passengers and freight to the land where "the rivers all run."